Passages Beyond the Gate

A Jungian Approach to Understanding American Psychology

George-Harold Jennings

University Press of America,® Inc.
Lanham · Boulder · New York · Toronto · Plymouth, UK

Copyright © 2010 by
University Press of America,® Inc.
4501 Forbes Boulevard
Suite 200
Lanham, Maryland 20706
UPA Acquisitions Department (301) 459-3366

Estover Road
Plymouth PL6 7PY
United Kingdom

Library of Congress Control Number: 2010929163
ISBN: 978-0-7618-5163-9 (paperback : alk. paper)
eISBN: 978-0-7618-5164-6

In loving memory of a matriarch:

Alice P. Jennings

was an exemplar of spiritual strength, wisdom, and purposeful living.

Contents

Prologue   vii

Acknowledgements   viii

Introduction   ix

Chapter 1 Exploring Passages that Reveal Human Nature:
A Student's Journey   1

Chapter 2 Jungian Ways of Knowing and the
Psychologies They Create   5

Chapter 3 The Role of the Inferior Function in
Jungian Psychology   23

Chapter 4 One of These Psychologies Is Unlike the Others   29

Chapter 5 Towards an American Psychology for All Psychological   35
Types

References   39

Index   43

About the Author   46

Prologue

Metaphorically speaking, there is a great wall that separates the material and secular views of human nature from a spiritual one in American psychology. Fortunately, the wall, though formidable in size, has a gate in it that remains barely ajar, the opening is just wide enough to allow spiritual knowledge to seep through from the other side. Travelers can observe several passages that mark the terrain leading up to the wall and the gate, but there the passages apparently end. Few observers or travelers along these pathways realize the roads actually connect to other passages beyond the gate. Although the gate is large and heavy, most of the travelers who pass by pay little attention to the barely opened gate. This remains the case because the object of their attention and admiration is the formidable size and impressive thickness of the wall. Other travelers who approach the barrier think about ways in which they can completely close the gate in order to cut off the flow of spiritual knowledge. Occasionally, travelers who approach the gate are intrigued by the flow from the other side. These travelers stop and look, and perhaps they even comment on what they see, but they eventually move on because they view the heaviness of the gate as a deterrent to observing more. "It's such a heavy gate!," they exclaim. It is probably much too hard to open further, and besides, moving it even slightly could result in personal injury. And then there are the remaining few travelers who are inquisitive and unyielding, and for whom a heavy gate serves not as a deterrent, but as a trigger that inspires them to act determinedly to summon the necessary strength to fully open the gate. As these travelers struggle mightily to open the gate wider, and ultimately to the widest degree possible, the following shared thought becomes etched upon their minds: "If we ever hope to complete the road map of human nature, we must not only travel and create passages on the familiar side of the gate, we must travel and create *Passages Beyond the Gate*."

Acknowledgements

The ideas presented in this book are the foundation of my doctoral dissertation, which was written many years ago. The inspiration and support I received from my psychology professors dating back to my undergraduate years have played a significant role in the birth and development of this treatise; consequently, I extend a heartfelt thank you to my Drew University undergraduate professors, Drs. Philip K. Jensen, James W. Mills, and Edward Domber, as well as to the members of my Pennsylvania State University dissertation committee, Drs. Juris Draguns (chair), Leon Gorlow, Richard M. Lundy, and Michael Smyer. Other professors of psychology who have strongly influenced my thoughts and feelings about psychology and human nature are Dr. Sidney J. Blatt of Yale School of Medicine and Dr. William J. Ray of Pennsylvania State University.

Emotionally and spiritually, supportive family, friends, and colleagues are among the greatest blessings one can have as one experiences the vicissitudes of everyday life. In this regard, I have been truly blessed by the presence of the following people in my life: Shirley M. Silver, Linda A. Smith, Keith A. Jennings, Michael-Robert Cheeks, Alicia Silver, Slater Jennings, Dr. Alpha O. Curry, Beverly Ross, Dr. Pauline Imbrigato, Dr. Lenore Wilkinson, William Jones, Alice Mathis, Alex Idavoy, Dr. LaFrancis Rodgers-Rose, Dr. N. Lynne Westfield, Jane Kourakis, Felipe Velez, the members of Drew University's Department of Psychology, the staff of Drew University's McClintock Center for Counseling and Psychological Services, and other members of the Drew University community too numerous to mention by name.

Intellectual inspiration and emotional and spiritual support are not the only things a writer hopes to receive when considering writing a book of this type. A writer also greatly benefits from positive and negative feedback from respected individuals, a mental focus that enables him or her to do very detailed and demanding work, and connections with other professionals willing and capable of doing the same. Again, I have been blessed in that I have been the beneficiary of all of the above, including the efforts put forth by the following editors and indexer who have played key roles in my being able to complete this work: Samantha Kirk, Kara Borbely, and Carol Frenier.

Introduction

Passages is a metaphor I use to identify the various theories psychologists, and especially personality theorists, have created that rely on traditional and respected quantitative, empirical methodologies, or theoretical formulations that have historically been acknowledged as important in our quest to describe and understand human nature. I refer of course to the classic writings of leading figures in Western psychological thought including William James (1902); John B. Watson (1913); Sigmund Freud (1963, 1966); Carl G. Jung (1923, 1931); Alfred Adler (1930, 1939); B. F. Skinner (1971, 1974); Karen Horney (1939, 1945); Abraham Maslow (1964, 1971); and Carl Rogers (1951, 1980). In addition, I speak of widely known and more contemporary theories in the field of cognitive-behavioral psychology including the writings of Albert Bandura (1977, 1989, 2006); Martin E. P. Seligman (1975); Arnold Lazarus (1971, 1973); and Aaron Beck (1972, 2005). I also refer to empirical research findings and theoretical ideas found in the works of some leading figures in the areas of positive psychology, for example, Martin E. P. Seligman and Mihaly Csikszentmihalyi (2000); Martin E. P. Seligman (2006), and biological psychology Hans Eysenck (1967, 1982); and David M. Buss (1990, 1991).

When a person studies psychology, he or she becomes a traveler along one or more of the various passages. While journeying along the passages, the traveler will be presented with compelling evidence that reveals human nature in specific ways. In addition, the experience of moving along any single passage may vary from person to person. It can range from the individual hating what she or he sees to loving it deeply, and being totally absorbed by the experience. As I suspect is the case with many who have read a textbook in psychology covering diverse methodologies and theoretical viewpoints, it does not take long before you know the theorists with whom you would like to explore ideas and who you would want to avoid.

As I reflect on my own journey along various passages, whenever I liked a theorist, I could easily imagine having long conversations into the late night hours with him or her. I had numerous imaginary conversations with Abraham Maslow and Carl Rogers as I came to realize how much I shared their view of the self-actualizing tendency in human beings. To me, Maslow and Rogers were warm and soothing. I also enjoyed the writings of Rollo May, who I wanted to sit with and have a cup of coffee on a bright and sunny day, in the belief that the sunshine would keep me more upbeat as we pondered the more challenging and negative forces with which most, if not all humans, are known to have to grapple.

B. F. Skinner, on the other hand, frustrated me. My early readings and attempts at understanding him left me wondering where exactly was the human side of human beings in his writings, as well as those of many other radical behaviorists. However, over time I came to realize that Skinner's viewpoint was extremely important and critical to the development of the discipline of psychology.

As we move into the second decade of the 21st century, American psychology largely advocates a secular and fundamentally materialistic viewpoint of the person. The realization of this fact has long troubled me. I am one who thinks it is important to view human beings as essentially spiritual in nature. Yet the more I studied psychology, the more I became aware that my core interests and developing viewpoint of human nature were closer to the periphery than the core of the discipline. Prior to applying to and attending graduate school, this growing awareness of the discipline's predominantly secular and materialistic viewpoint of the person compelled me to ask, "Is psychology really for me?" I wondered if I should instead pursue a career in religious studies, philosophy, social work, or another related field. I was looking for a graduate student experience and eventually a career opportunity that would readily allow me to fully understand the importance of human transcendence as the concept was studied and discussed by Abraham Maslow (1964, 1971). In Maslow's writings, transcendence is strongly linked to spirituality. I wanted to understand transcendence, spiritually, and related concepts (e.g., peak experiences (Maslow, 1964, 1971)) intellectually and emotionally, the manner in which these things were experienced by others, and how they might also be experienced by me. Ultimately, it was a profound interest in humanistic-existential psychology, an unyielding interest in clinical psychology, and in the practice of psychotherapy that prevented me from pursuing a career in another area, even though I knew my deepest interests remained foreign to most psychologists.

Graduating from college with the immediate goal of going straight into a doctoral degree graduate program was indeed an exciting period in my life. A new phase of life was about to begin for me; I welcomed it. Yet I had no idea just how potent the experience that was about to unfold would become, nor did I foresee the opportunities it would bring to the forefront, which would ultimately give me a deeper sense of dynamic processes in the discipline of American psychology that underlie its evolution.

It was not until I attended graduate school at The Pennsylvania State University and started an internship in clinical psychology at Yale School of Medicine that I began to see a noteworthy pattern of development within the field of American psychology. This pattern seemingly compelled the growth of the discipline at the expense of interests that were most dear to me and others with whom I found common ground. My graduate work took me deep into the thinking of Carl G. Jung, and this in turn fed a growing awareness in me of the importance of several of his ideas. Eventually, Jung's ideas were the key to my understanding of what was happening in American psychology.

Walking through the model of psychological development found in Jungian psychology, I could attempt to offer an explanation regarding why certain theories exist, and why they become a part of mainstream American psychology while other theories do not. Within the pages of this book you will find a description and explanation of what I came to realize.

A review of most books in psychology, especially those focused on theories of personality as the subject matter, reveals attempts by many authors or theorists to describe, analyze, or interpret human nature. American psychologists take pride in the genius of their pioneers (e.g., William James, John B. Watson, B. F. Skinner, Albert Bandura, Abraham Maslow, Carl Rogers) and the individuals who followed in their footsteps. Yet the indelible impact of Sigmund Freud and other European theorists is apparent to even those American psychologists who do not support their views.

The early to mid 20th century pioneers created or adopted various methodologies, which have greatly influenced the form and content of today's mainstream American psychology. These researchers and theoreticians have been effective in that they offered a strong understanding of human nature grounded in behavioral, psychoanalytic, cognitive-behavioral, humanistic-existential, and–in certain periods of our past–biological thought and research that existed prior to the more contemporary biological psychology, which students are able to study today. Still, the above statement compels one to take note of one of mainstream American psychology's most apparent weaknesses: namely its failure to accept or develop a spiritually imbued psychology.

In my view, we must redress the stunning paucity of psychological knowledge regarding the spiritual nature of human beings. While mainstream American psychology seems quite willing to embrace the explosive biological view of human beings, which draws psychology closer and closer to a materialistic understanding of what it means to be human, a strikingly unbalanced viewpoint of the person is the inevitable outcome of our current dominant research trends and intellectual pursuits. To help correct this imbalance, in this work I propose that American psychologists act to strongly embrace, and ultimately integrate, spiritual concepts and ways of understanding human nature with our more traditional ways of exploring human nature. Moreover, I propose these actions take place to the fullest degree that is possible in all sub-disciplines of psychology, but most prominently in the field of personality. I encourage psychologists to extend or broaden the discussion of spirituality in the classroom and in other settings where psychological ideas are discussed. I encourage psychologists to do greater research on spirituality, as well as to address the issue of spirituality in the discipline's major textbooks and other types of psychological literature.

If you happen to be thinking, "Why place a major focus on personality?," consider the following: as a field of study, personality is a natural place to begin one's quest for a comprehensive psychological understanding of human nature because, although it may not be viewed as such by all psychologists, the field of personality remains the centerpiece of the discipline of psychology. This statement is consistent with thoughts expressed by distinguished psychologist Walter Mischel (1976), who states:

> The field of personality is at the crossroads of most areas of psychology: it is the point of convergence between the study of human development and change, of abnormality and deviance as well as of competence and fulfillment, of emotions and thought, of learning and social relations. The breath of the field is not surprising because for many psychologists the object of personality study has been nothing less than the total person. (p. 2)[1]

As one who has taught courses in introduction to psychology, small group dynamics, abnormal psychology, theories of personality, and various other psychology related seminars over the years, the most profound and meaningful questions raised by students, and the most thoughtful answers I have been able to give in response to their questions, always have related fundamentally to issues having to do with personality.

I have looked forward to the day when *Passages Beyond the Gate* would be published as a monograph. Now, given that the day has arrived, it is my hope that readers of this work will: 1) view it as having offered a new and meaningful way of examining why different personality theories have merged or emerged as psychological forces within American psychology; 2) gain an understanding regarding why the forces have come forth or unfolded in a somewhat predictable sequence; and 3) see why each force has expressed itself more or less powerfully in relation to other forces in ways that presently shape the character of American psychology.

Is there long-term value in viewing personality theories and psychological forces under the proposed broad headings and categories presented in this work? I certainly think so, and I hope you will agree; however, if nothing more, I trust you will experience this work as a meaningful contribution to the ongoing intellectual discussions regarding the value of exploring spirituality more fully across all centers and places of learning that today lend themselves to the evolving character of American psychology.

Notes

1.   Introduction to Personality. (1976). New York: Holt, Rinehart and Winston, Inc.

Chapter 1
Exploring Passages that Reveal Human Nature:
A Student's Journey

"It would be so much simpler if I knew nothing; but I know too much, through my ancestors and my own education."
Carl G. Jung *Analytical Psychology: Its Theory and Practice*

My journey towards a PhD in psychology began when I declared psychology as my major while an undergraduate student in the College of Liberal Arts at Drew University. After earning my baccalaureate from Drew, I attended graduate school at The Pennsylvania State University in University Park, Pennsylvania. My area of concentration was clinical psychology. Following a three-year stay at Penn State, during which time I earned a master's degree and completed my comprehensive examinations, I began my preparation for an internship in clinical psychology. I was fortunate; I was granted a fellowship to fund an internship year at the institution I most favored. On July 1, 1979, I began a dynamic 12-month internship in clinical psychology at Yale School of Medicine in New Haven, Connecticut. In addition to starting the internship, I was ready to begin work on my dissertation. As an undergraduate I was fascinated by psychology. As a graduate student I continued to be highly intrigued by the insights I gained into human nature as a result of my ongoing, and now considerably advanced, studies in the discipline. During the three years between graduating from college and starting the internship at Yale, I immersed myself in an intensive study of humanistic-existential psychology, an immersion that had its roots in my experience as an undergraduate at Drew. I also began a deep exploration into Jungian psychology, having found a few professors at Penn State with either a passing or deeper interest in the man and his works. During the mid 1970's, the psychology faculty at Penn State featured several of the leading theorists and researchers in the country in the area of behavioral psychology and cognitive–behavioral psychology. These researchers cemented the school's reputation as a premier institution to study these approaches to psychology. Although I found them intriguing on some levels, I was not a strong proponent of behavioral or cognitive-behavioral approaches.

I continued to grow in my overall understanding of psychological factors that contribute to healthy and unhealthy ways of human functioning while a graduate student at Penn State. I credit some of that growth to working through my personal struggles given my early unwillingness to accept many of the tenets of behavioral psychology and cognitive-behavioral psychology. With this stage of personal struggle behind me, I looked forward to going to Yale Medical School to continue my journey towards the goal of becoming a psychologist while, perhaps along the way, grasping a more complete understanding of human psychological functioning. Shortly following my arrival, I realized that I was not going to be disappointed.

In addition to the Department of Psychology in the Graduate School, Yale had a psychology section in the Department of Psychiatry in the Medical School. Several diverse theoretical perspectives were taught in the psychology section by clinical supervisors and Yale University faculty. I felt most of the psychologists who supervised my work and taught me were considerably more open to and appreciative of psychoanalytic approaches, especially in ways which Pine (1988) might describe as consistent with "the four psychologies of psychoanalysis;" namely, "(a) drive, (b) ego, (c) object-relations, and (d) self-psychological meaning" (Yarock, 1993). I found this rather exciting. Consequently, I welcomed the opportunity to explore the ideas that comprised the systems of thought known as neo-Freudian psychology (e.g., Horney, 1945); ego psychology (e.g., Freud, A., 1946), and object relations theory (e.g., Kohut, 1977). I was expecting this to be a new and different way to explore psychology, and that turned out to be true.

At Yale I found myself traveling along a different psychological road, which was different from other psychological pathways I had taken towards the goal of understanding human nature. As an undergrad, I felt highly stimulated intellectually and personally liberated by the writings of Carl Rogers, Abraham Maslow, and Rollo May. In graduate school, I began to see the value of the behavioral and cognitive-behavioral approaches, although I was unable to develop a passionate interest in them. With this background going into the internship program, I found my increasing exposure to object relations theory and related psychoanalytic concepts extremely valuable, but this exposure contributed to a growing feeling of concern and frustration I had regarding the value that the different institutions I had attended (or knew of through friends and colleagues) placed on the major and sometimes competing psychological approaches to understanding human nature. By the late fall of 1979, I certainly knew what I liked in psychology and what I did not. Many of the theories had beckoned to me, but I felt some of them did not provide me with a strong enough sense of what it truly means to be human. I sincerely felt some of the theories had missed the mark. There was something about human beings, something that was at our core, indeed essential to human nature that few of the theories demonstrated an ability to capture. In my view, human spirituality was insufficiently being addressed in the writings of most psychologists, and especially by those persons considered mainstream psychologists.

My strong interest in humanistic-existential psychology and psychodynamic psychology, my general frustration with behavioral approaches, and mixed appreciation for some of the cognitive-behavioral approaches revealed a major schism within me. The schisms also surrounded me because they were actually in the discipline as well. Questions arose. I wondered why such schisms existed in psychology? Why did I encounter colleagues and psychologists at Yale who clearly were interested in psychoanalytic psychologies, while they rarely said a word about behavioral or humanistic-existential perspectives? It was not the case that other perspectives were never discussed, for at least one of my supervisors discussed multiple perspectives with me while under her supervision. Rather, relative to my experience at other institutions, it seemed that greater significance was placed on psychoanalytic understanding. The situation was reversed at Penn State where behavioral and cognitive-behavioral approaches were assigned the highest value in the department and other approaches were granted secondary status, tertiary status, or no status at all.

Having had some exposure to the writings of Carl Jung, I found the manner in which American psychology dealt with Jungian psychology intriguing. Jung's relatively weak influence on mainstream American psychology compelled me to ask, "Why was Jungian psychology–a psychology with powerful spiritual overtones–mentioned, but assigned fairly low status within the discipline?" I wondered, "Were American psychologists quite simply determined to downplay or deny the spiritual nature of human beings?" I embarked on a search to uncover the meaning, value, and purpose of spirituality in psychology. My intellectual grappling with these concerns led to my reflecting on Jung's account of the reasons why he disagreed with Sigmund Freud and Alfred Adler regarding their understanding of human nature. Freud, Adler, and Jung were different psychological types; that is to say, they held fundamentally different and/or competing ideas about human nature. Jung's psychological theory attempted to account for these different and opposing viewpoints regarding the same phenomena. Although I had never seen it expressed as such, there was–applying a Jungian concept–clearly a psychological type problem in American psychology, and I was probably one of many students who was forced to struggle with its consequences.

There are many theories that comprise American psychology. The theories range from the more scientific behavioral, cognitive-behavioral, cognitive, and biological (including neuropsychological) approaches to the various psychodynamic, humanistic, existential approaches. These theories are more or less presented in the mainstream literature that comprises American psychology; but being accepted within the mainstream does not mean a lack of competition among the theories. In American psychology, some mainstream theories are more highly valued than others and a clash among some of the theoretical viewpoints continues to exist. As a student in psychology, I was subject to having to deal with these competing viewpoints, which were expressed at the highest levels of the discipline. Ultimately, my attempt to understand the dynamics underlying the conflict between theories and/or the development of competing psychological perspectives regarding the study of human beings resulted in my doctoral dissertation (Jennings, 1982). In it I explored the relationship between the Jungian psychological functions that underlie psychological type and the so-called "four forces in American psychology" (Sutich, 1969).

I had traveled many passages hoping to find the one way that would reveal the most accurate information about what it means to be human. Intellectually, I was searching for a way of understanding human nature that would include a complete or whole picture of the person in American psychology. By way of an application of concepts germane to Jungian psychology, I came across a means of identifying why such a goal may or may not be possible. I revealed what I thought was the answer in my dissertation; several years later it resulted in my writing this book.

Chapter 2
Jungian Ways of Knowing and the Psychologies They Create[1]

"The present day shows with appalling clarity how little able people are to let the other man's argument count . . ."
Carl G. Jung *The Structure and Dynamics of the Psyche*

In his research on psychological types, Jung stressed the importance of two distinct conscious attitudes, which he identified as extraversion and introversion. Jung's classic definition of the two attitudes still stands out as the most informative to be found in the psychological literature. Regarding extraversion he writes (1923):

> Extraversion means an outward-turning of the libido (q.v.). With this concept I denote a manifest relatedness of the subject to object in the sense of a positive movement of subjective interest towards the object. Everyone in the state of extraversion thinks, feels, and acts in relation to the object, and moreover in a direct and clearly observable fashion so that no doubt can exist about his positive dependence upon the object. In a sense, therefore, extraversion is an outgoing transference of interest from the subject to the object . . . Should the state of extraversion become habitual, the *extraverted type* (v. Type) appears. (p. 543)

In his effort to convey his meaning of introversion, he states:

> Introversion means a turning inwards of the libido (q.v.) whereby a negative relation of the subject to object is expressed. Interest does not move towards the object, but recedes toward the subject. Everyone whose attitude is introverted, thinks, feels, and acts in a way that clearly demonstrates that the subject is the chief factor of motivation while the object at most receives only a secondary value. . . . When introversion is habitual, one speaks of an introverted type (v. Type). (p. 567)

Further research led Jung to isolate what he described as the four functions of consciousness. He identified these as sensing, intuiting, thinking, and feeling (Jung, 1923, 1931). Deeper consideration led him to group the functions into two categories. He specified sensing and intuiting as irrational or purely perceptual functions and he specified thinking and feeling as rational or judgmental functions. The four functions of consciousness are commonly depicted diagrammatically as shown in Figure 2-1.

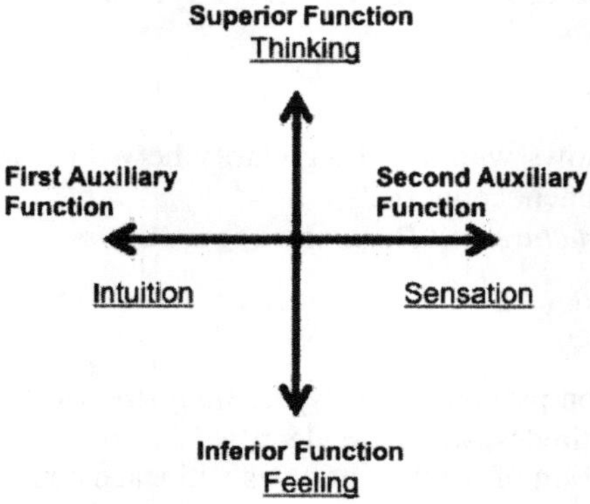

Superior Function
Thinking

First Auxiliary
Function

Second Auxiliary
Function

Intuition   Sensation

Inferior Function
Feeling

Figure 2-1 An aspect of the fourfold structure of the psyche depicting a possible arrangement of the psychological functions.

In the above example, thinking is in opposition to feeling and intuition is in opposition to sensation. A clearer understanding of each function's purpose is detailed in the writings of Jung and many persons influenced by him (e.g., Gray and Wheelwright, 1944, 1945; von Franz, 1971). At this point, a review of the meaning Jung gave each function will serve to enhance understanding.

The Evaluative Functions: Thinking and Feeling

According to Jung, thinking is the intellectual function par excellence. Through the use of this function, the person acts to organize the world along the lines of certain principles and theories that aim at creating intellectual objectivity. Thinking is a judgmental process that interprets or tells us what an action or behavior means. The thinking function is the most rational facet of consciousness. When thinking strongly influences the consciousness of an individual, the person becomes keen in the acts of generating systematic formulations, identifying linear causality, and organizing, interpreting, and classifying information.

Feeling is the polar opposite of thinking; yet it too is judgmental. However, unlike thinking's intellectual objectivity, feeling is guided by a more subjective component in that it generates opinions or declares what is liked and/or disliked. The feeling function permits the person to judge the value or worth of things; and it permits us to state our views on the things that we feel are important to us. Some things are judged to be good while others are judged to be bad. Other feeling terms include the words wonderful, ugly, depressing, and beautiful. Among the values we are likely to consider very important are freedom, beauty, and justice.

The expression of feelings reflects the individual's value system. Many persons are inclined to believe that feelings and emotions are identical, but they are not equivalent–as shall be noted shortly. A strong linkage to the value system gives feelings their subjective quality. As a judgmental function, feelings are capable of judging emotional states, just like they are capable of judging a painting or person. One way emotions differ from feelings is that emotions do not evaluate. The emotional or physiological state of anger may exist, but it is feeling that informs us we are angry. Jung (1923) writes, "when the intensity of feeling is increased an affect results" (p. 544). Emotions and affects are more like each other in nature than are emotions and feelings according to Jung's use of the terms. In common language usage however, people generally use these three terms interchangeably. When feelings strongly influence the consciousness of the individual, the result may be a person who is drawn to passionate and highly subjective modes of expression. The expressions are often critical statements of the things he values about himself and/or other things in the world.

The Perceptual Functions: Intuition and Sensation

The conscious function intuition gives one the ability to have deep insight into the nature of things. Intuition permits one to delve into the intrinsic nature of an object or discern the inner qualities of a situation. It puts one in touch with the essential purpose of things or situations, as well as their various possibilities. When intuition strongly influences the consciousness of the individual, the result may be a person who is attracted to mysteries or has frequent mystical experiences. The person may be a visionary among men and women, for they are frequently though inextricably, linked to unknown realms. "The intuitive function . . . provides us with startling inspirations, revelations and insights regarding what is not readily observable but is nevertheless true" (O'Connell and O'Connell, 1974, p. 281). This is strikingly different from its polar opposite function sensation, which enables us to know what a thing is, that is, it establishes the existence of an object and allows one to describe it. By means of sensation, we know a book is an object of a certain weight, color, texture, or size. There is nothing about the sensation function that permits one to go beyond a description or the mere appearance of the book. Sensation is called the reality function. When the sensation-dominated person perceives a book, the many different purposes for which the book may be used rarely enter his mind. The sensing person is foremost interested in the facts about the book, and the most important fact is that it exists. He knows the book exists because he can touch it, see it, or use any of his other senses to verify its existence. When sensations strongly influence the consciousness of the individual, the result is a person who is a master of observation, a person who notices everything. Sensation is the function that is identical to perception as the term is commonly used.

How the Functions Operate

Jung believed that it is not possible to use the evaluative functions thinking and feeling simultaneously; nor did he believe that the perceptual functions could be used at the same time. He argued that the process of switching from thinking to feeling or intuiting to sensing may be so rapid that individuals may believe they perform opposing functions simultaneously.

In Figure 2-1, thinking is placed at the position of the superior function. This implies that thinking (in this particular case) is the most highly developed or dominating function. As the superior function, thinking would be expected to operate quite well, and it is likely to be more efficient in its action than any of the other functions. If Figure 2-1 were to represent the way consciousness is organized within an individual, this person would be viewed as strongly thinking oriented. It is quite possible that such a person would tend to rely on his thinking function even though he finds himself in situations that actually call for the use of the feeling function. This person would have difficulty using his feeling function to its fullest, since by definition the function opposing the superior function is generally in the most undeveloped state. Jung would call the feeling function in this person his inferior function.

When the need arises for the functions to perform, the inferior function rarely seems to operate properly. Often it seems to be disassociated from the other functions and, apparently, unable to operate in harmony with them. The inferior function is often devalued for this reason. When the occasions arise to evaluate objects or situations, the highly thinking-oriented person will have a tendency to rely more and more upon the thinking function. As he becomes more dependent on its use to the near exclusion of the use of the feeling function or the other functions, he gradually molds himself into a thinking-type. Unable to use his inferior function deliberately and effectively, the thinking-type may eventually develop one of the perceptual functions as an auxiliary or helping function.

The auxiliaries normally ensure a greater grasp of reality in terms of personal understanding; that is, they aid the person by helping him discern the external manifold, or the inner world of personal, subjective experience. If a perceptual function were the superior function, the auxiliaries would by definition be evaluative functions. The auxiliary function that the person is most inclined to use to assist the superior function is termed the first auxiliary function. This function in some cases may attain a state of development equal to, or only slightly less influential than, that of the superior function. In Figure 2-1, the first auxiliary function is intuition. A person who typically depends on thinking, backed up by a rather strong intuitive function, may be classified as an intuitive-thinking type. The second auxiliary function will develop after the first auxiliary function, but it may have greater difficulty reaching a similar state of development as the first auxiliary.

The inferior or fourth function generally remains the most problematic function for the individual–the person may lose effective control over its realm of operation. Jung stated that much of the inferior function operates unconsciously. What we find among sophisticated and highly developed persons is two or three conscious functions that work in harmony (generally a superior function and one, but optimally two, effective auxiliaries) and one seemingly disassociated function.

The four functions, in part, reflect the fourfold structure of the psyche. For Jung this was an important discovery.

> In studying the behavior of his patients, he found, he had apparently hit upon a basic structure of the psyche. Naturally, the basic fourfold structure of the psyche, which means more than only the conscious functions, is generally represented as a purely primitive self-manifestation of the unconscious, usually as an undifferentiated quaternion. There are just four principles of more or less the same kind: four colours, or angles, or gods, etc. The more they are connected with consciousness, the more they tend to become three animals, and one human being, or three good gods and one evil god . . . Neither in psychology nor any other field of reality is there ever a onesided course of action, for if the unconscious builds up a field of consciousness, the repercussion of such a change produces an alteration in the unconscious structure as well. (von Franz, 1971, p. 2)

There are three great forces or movements in American psychology, and a fourth force or movement that most mainstream American psychologists know very little or nothing about. Many mainstream American psychologists who are told about the subject matter of the fourth movement completely reject it as a meaningful or desirable psychology. The three great forces are the behavioral, psychoanalytic, and humanistic-existential perspectives, and the fourth force or movement is the transpersonal perspective (Maslow, 1968). In theory, this fourth force could conceivably attain greatness in American psychology. In consideration of Jung's concept of the fourfold structure of consciousness, it makes sense that there should be four great psychological forces. Whether this is absolutely the case perhaps can neither be confirmed nor disproved. What can be demonstrated, however, is whether or not there is a strong relationship between the four psychological forces identified above and the four Jungian functions.

The theoretical analysis in this treatise is focused on establishing the relationship between the so-called four forces within American psychology–behavioral, psychoanalytic, humanistic-existential, and transpersonal–and the four Jungian functions. The initial clue as to how these four psychological forces should be paired with the four Jungian functions was suggested by a reading of Marie-Louise von Franz who wrote: "Jung never said anything about Freud's type as a human being, he only pointed out in his books that Freud's *system* represents extraverted thinking" (1971, p. 49). This comment suggests that Jung recognized the pattern and influences of the thinking function in Freudian psychoanalysis.

In this work, the thinking function is paired with psychoanalytic psychology. The common emphasis on values leads to the theoretical pairing of the feeling function and humanistic-existential psychology. With observation, and a greater concern with describing the object as opposed to making inferences about it as a major focal point, the sensation function is logically paired with behavioral psychology. This leaves the intuitive function to be paired with transpersonal psychology. The link is sound when one considers that many of the ideas that permeate transpersonal thought are decidedly intuitively derived, particularly those having to do with its "spiritual paths."

Behavioral Psychology and the Sensation Function

Mischel (1976) and Maddi (1976) divide behavioral theories into separate camps within the larger behavioral movement. In addition to the radical behaviorism of Watson and Skinner, there is the behavioral psychology represented by the work of Hull (1943), Spence (1948), and Dollard and Miller (1950). Their moderate form of behaviorism "derives in essence from the pioneering work of Ivan P. Pavlov" (Maddi, 1976, p. 534) and comprises the moderate camp. A third aspect of the behavioral movement consists of a group of psychologists known as the cognitive-behavioral theorists or social learning theorists.

Radical behavioral psychology reflects a scientific position wherein the sensation function has reached the ascendancy and there appears to be little contamination by the other functions. Indeed, the nature of this psychology was firmly established by Watson, whose definitive opening sentence in his widely read article "Psychology as the Behaviorist Views It" was: "Psychology as the behaviorist views it is a purely objective experimental branch of natural science" (Watson, 1913, p. 158). Radical behavioral psychology resists making assumptions about the nature of things intangible to the senses. "What is called 'methodological behaviorism' limits itself to what can be publicly observed; mental processes may exist, but they are ruled out of scientific consideration by their nature" (Skinner, 1971, p. 190).

Maddi (1976) reports a carefully worded explanation for the "methodological procedure" characteristic of behaviorism:

> For the radical behaviorist, one gains nothing of scientific value in "explaining" that a person eats at one time and not at another by saying that he was hungry at first and not subsequently. One gains nothing because it is then necessary to determine the mechanisms governing the waxing and waning of whatever it is that is called hunger. This turns out to be number of hours since last having eaten. It is this tangible, observable, external stimulus situation that governs eating behavior. To talk of a hunger drive is at best superfluous (if we know the external stimuli controlling the responses to be explained) and at worst misleading (by dulling our curiosity to find the external stimuli if we do not yet know them). (p. 553)

It is clear that many behavioral theorists emphasize, in fact glorify, the role of observation. Only those things that are clearly discernable to the senses are appropriate subject matter for study by radical behavioral psychologists.

Bandura and Walters (1963) and Rotter (1966) are among the primary advocates of the scientific study of cognitive processes and behavior. Although they too value observation, their cognitive-behavioral position is unique within the behavioral movement in that many of the proponents of this theory are grappling with a viewpoint of the person that encompasses the relationship between awareness, learning, and the person's self-regulating and self-controlling behaviors.

In discussing the sensation function, it should be noted that one of its most salient features is that it produces a person who is interested in the facts, the observable, and that which is most easily verifiable. Walter Mischel (1976), commenting on modern behavioral theories and their application, writes:

> Application of current social behavior theory focuses on selected, carefully defined behaviors and the observable stimulus conditions that seem to covary with them. One tries to observe what the person does, rather than to infer what he has or is. The search is for the stimulus conditions controlling or causing particular behavior patterns; one does not try to interpret the behaviors as indirect signs of the person's underlying motives and dispositions. For this purpose behavioral assessments seek to specify objectivity the response patterns of interest, and to identify relevant stimulus conditions. (p. 199)

In maintaining a stance that is congruent with the nature of the sensation function, behavioral scientists have developed a psychology that relies primarily on the perception of highly visible phenomena, that is, behavior and other concrete data of human experience. Behavioral perspectives have not emerged to be superficial nor demanding of concrete data in a disparaging way; however, many opponents of radical behavioral psychology have resorted to attacking these psychological approaches because of their strong, and in the case of radical behaviorism, unyielding emphasis on the observable.

Sensation-oriented persons are inclined to place great emphasis on the tangible and the observable; however, this is not particularly the case with persons more in tune with the other three functions. Given the way Jung defines intuition, one can imagine the difficulty a highly intuitive person would have in his struggles to accept a psychology exclusively based on the concretely observable and tangible. A highly intuitive person would attempt to get a perceptual impression of what was behind the facade of the observable; such a person would continually try to get at the more hidden essence or underlying features of the object or situation under study. Furthermore, imagine the difficulty the thinking- or feeling-oriented person would have being content with what Mischel states as observing "what the person does, rather than infer what he has or is." Making inferences about objects and situations is as natural to evaluative functions as perception is to the sensation function.

The data that are most readily apparent to the senses are quite important, and nowhere is this importance shown with greater emphasis than in behavioral approaches. At present, behavioral approaches with their close ties to positivistic science are the most powerful force in American psychology. Behavioral psychology's close relationship with the sensation function adds strength to the argument that the sensation function is the most dominant function in American psychology and thus should be noted as its superior function.

Psychoanalytic Psychology[2] and the Thinking Function

Many of the principles and concepts to be found in psychoanalytic psychology derive not from direct sensory observation, but from observation in combination with a powerful extension of the rational thought process (thinking). Psychoanalytically oriented psychology represents highly systematic attempts at articulating the processes underlying manifest behavior, as well as what the behavior means. Its emphasis is on meaning, interpretation, organization, the linear sequence of events and their effects, and its ever-increasing legion of concepts and categories, elevates psychoanalytic psychology to the stature of a thinking-oriented psychology that is without equal among all psychologies in the United States. Maslow (1968) and Sutich (1969) view psychoanalytic psychology as the second force or movement in American psychology.

The psychologies comprising this movement can be separated into multiple camps. First and foremost is psychoanalysis, the prototype of the psychoanalytic psychologies. A second camp of psychoanalytically oriented psychologies consists of the writings of a group of theorists known as the neo-Freudian social theorists, and a third camp consists of persons known as the neo-Freudian ego theorists. Other camps include theorists devoted to writing about object relations theory, and self-theory. The alignment of a given theorist with either the neo-Freudian social, ego, object relations, or self camp is not absolute; nevertheless, theorists such as Erich Fromm, Karen Horney, and Harry Stack Sullivan are noted for their emphasis on sociocultural factors, while theorists such as Heinz Hartmann and David Rapaport are noted for their emphasis on the ego, its functions, and its development. Erik Erickson is also interested in ego development as well as social development, and thus could be included in either camp. The theories of the above-named persons form the basis of the psychoanalytic movement. The theories of Alfred Adler, Carl Jung, and Otto Rank have their roots in psychoanalytic thought; however, the work of these important psychodynamic theorists includes such striking derivations away from Freud's more essential concepts that their theories, for the most part, fall outside the boundaries of the psychoanalytic movement.

Thinking is a function characterized by organization, categorization, systematization, linear process, and so forth. Maddi (1976) comments, "This activity is generally referred to as determining what something means" (p. 305). Fine (1973) writes that psychoanalysis is a process that "assumes that everything is meaningful." Freud called this the principle of psychic determination (p. 7). Like the other three major psychological movements, psychoanalysis represents an attempt at developing a model of the person that reflects a total approach to the person. Psychoanalysis has been defined as: (1) a procedure for investigating unconscious mental processes (a procedure deemed possible through the inferential quality of the thinking function); (2) a method of psychotherapy used to treat neurotic disorder through the use of free association, relying on the analysis of transference and resistance; and (3) a procedure for gathering additional psychological information for the development of the science of psychoanalysis (Fine, 1973). Thinking reaches a high level of expression in psychoanalytic psychology, but the system itself–highly sophisticated and strongly inferential–has also met with severe criticism. Proponents of the behavioral models could hardly make a better argument about the limitations of psychoanalytic psychology than does the psychoanalyst Kubie (1953), who writes:

> The difficulties of recording and reproducing primary observations, the consequent difficulty in deriving the basic conceptual structure, the difficulties in examining with equal ease the circular relationship from unconscious to conscious and from conscious to unconscious, the difficulties in appraising quantitatively the multiplicity of variables and finally the difficulties of estimating those things which increase and those things which decrease the precision of its hypotheses and the validity of its hypotheses and the validity of its predictions are among the basic scientific problems which remain to be solved. (pp. 143-144)

Proponents of the behavioral models not wishing to get caught up in the ethereal thinking world of psychoanalytic psychology often react strongly to what they view as a lack of verifiable thinking-derived constructs inherent to this approach. Where sensation-oriented psychologists see a lack of true objectivity as a major problem with psychoanalysis, many proponents of both the humanistic and transpersonal approaches (which here are associated with the feeling and intuitive functions, respectively) have not refrained from citing what they view to be the shortcomings of this explicatory approach. In feeling (value-laden) terms, humanistic, third-force psychologists have written that psychoanalytic psychology is a cold, pessimistic, and mechanical psychological approach to the study of the person. Many humanistic psychologists react to the emphasis on linear-process causality that underlies psychoanalytic thought. A strong belief in linear-process causality generally leads one to focus on the past. Humanistic psychologists are much more focused on the present, and they typically reject psychoanalytic psychologists' emphasis on determinism.

Many advocates of transpersonal approaches are disenchanted with psychoanalytic psychology because the system lacks spirituality. The mystical, oceanic, and related psi experiences are frequently explained away as irrational preoccupations of the individual. As a theory of culture, psychoanalysis has even sought to explain widespread belief in God or a God-Force as based essentially on wish fulfillment rather than on reality.

In spite of these criticisms, the powerful influence the combined psychoanalytic approach has upon the whole of American psychology cannot be denied. Yet its impact continues to fall short of the impact the sensation-oriented approach (including the behavioral, cognitive-behavioral, and biological psychologies) has upon American psychology. Psychoanalytic psychology's close relatedness with the thinking function gives strength to the argument that the thinking function is the second most dominant function in American psychology; and thus, it should be noted as American psychology's first auxiliary function.

Humanistic-Existential Psychology and the Feeling Function

In 1962, Abraham Maslow issued the following proclamation to the American psychological community:

> There is now emerging over the horizon a new conception of human sickness, and of human health, a psychology that I find so thrilling and so full of wonderful possibilities that I yield to the temptation to present it publicly even before it is checked and confirmed, and before it can be called reliable scientific knowledge. (p. 3)

In Jungian terms, Maslow's proclamation marked a large-scale differentiation of the feeling function in the psyche of American psychology. The feeling function had proclaimed the results of the evaluation of the person, and it had found human nature to be "neutral, premoral, or positively 'good'" (Maslow, 1962, p. 3). Humanistic psychology was soon received as the third force in American psychology. Its followers came to view as part of this psychology's goal the restoration of dignity to the individual. This was to be achieved by emphasizing holism and synthesis as opposed to analysis. The movement also saw as its goal the search or renewed search for human values. It emphasized individual uniqueness, freedom, and aesthetics. Thinking-oriented persons frequently discredit humanistic psychology for its weak attempts at systematization and organization. Sensation-oriented persons fault it for its subjectivity and lack of scientific rigor, which are the same criticisms they have regarding the psychoanalytic and transpersonal approaches.

Humanistic psychology mirrors the highly differentiated positive expression of the feeling function:

> It stands for the respect for the worth of persons, respect for differences of approaches, open-mindedness as to acceptable methods, and interest in exploration of new aspects of human behavior. As a "third force" in contemporary psychology it is concerned with topics having little place in existing theories and systems: e.g., love, creativity, self growth, organism, basic need-gratification, self-actualization, higher values, being, becoming, spontaneity, play humor, affection, naturalness, warmth, ego-transcendence, objectivity, autonomy, responsibility, meaning, fair-play, transcendental experience, peak experience, courage, and related concepts. (Sutich, 1963, mimeo.)

The negative, though equally differentiated, expression of this function permeates much of the existential psychology that has come to influence American psychology. Existential thought originated in Europe, whereas humanistic psychology is American in origin. Although the approaches have many similarities, the American approach is full of "optimism and limitless horizons" and

> The European focus is on the tragic dimensions of existence, on limits, on facing and taking into oneself the anxiety of uncertainty and nonbeing. The humanistic psychologist, on the other hand, speaks less of limits and contingency than of development of potential, less of acceptance than of awareness, less of anxiety than of peak experiences and oceanic oneness, less of life meaning than self-realization, less of apartness and basic isolation than I-thou and encounter. (Yalom, 1977, pp. 60-61)

Now, and perhaps for several years to come, the subject matter of humanistic-existential psychology and transpersonal psychology will overlap to some degree. As humanistic-existential psychology continues to develop its scope, it will become more distinct from subject matter more likely to be explored in transpersonal psychology. The beginning of the construction of dividers between the two approaches can be noted in the writings of Kinget (1975), who offers one of the first systematic approaches to understanding and applying humanistic psychology. She writes:

> Although humanistic psychology focuses on the fullest expression of the human phenomenon and does not exclude anything pertinent to the human venture, its compass does not extend beyond the confines of the human order. It does include the study of religious behavior and experience–both of which have historically been among the most characteristic expressions of human specific-

ity. But these are natural, not supernatural, phenomena. Humanistic psychology is open even to the preternatural–that is, to observations and reports not explainable by currently known theories and laws. However, extraordinary phenomena are not the focus of humanistic psychology. And the supernatural is distinctly outside the province of this psychology. (Kinget, 1975, p. 165)

Humanistic-existential psychology is closely aligned with the value-oriented feeling function. Compared to the sensation-oriented behavioral psychology and the thinking-oriented psychoanalytic psychology, this relative newcomer, though influential, still struggles from time to time for the same degree of recognition enjoyed by the first two forces in American psychology. Within the psyche of American psychology, the feeling function, which expresses itself through this third movement, should be noted as American psychology's second auxiliary function.

Transpersonal Psychology and the Intuitive Function

Transpersonal psychology is a remarkably complex area of study. Anthony Sutich writes in the first issue of the *Journal of Transpersonal Psychology* (1969):

> Transpersonal Psychology is the title given to an emerging force in the psychology field by a group of psychologists and professional men and women from other fields who are interested in those ultimate human capacities and potentialities that have no systematic place in positivistic or behavioral theory ("first force"), classical psychoanalytic theory ("second force"), or humanistic psychology ("third force"). The emerging transpersonal psychology ("fourth force") is concerned specifically with the empirical, scientific study of, and responsible implementation of the findings relevant to, becoming, individual and species-wide meta-needs, ultimate values, unitive consciousness, peak experiences, B-Values, ecstasy, mystical experience, awe, being, self-actualization, essence, bliss, wonder, ultimate meaning, transcendence of the self, spirit, oneness, cosmic awareness, individual and species-wide synergy, maximal interpersonal encounter, sacralization of everyday life, transcendental phenomena, cosmic self-humor and playfulness, maximal sensory awareness, responsiveness and expression, and related concepts, experiences, and activities. As a definition, this formulation is to be understood as subject to optimal individual or group interpretations, either wholly or in part, with regard to the acceptance of its content as essentially naturalistic, theistic, supernaturalistic, or any other designated classification. (Preface)

Methodological transpersonal psychology explores novel realms, mystical realms (i.e., psi phenomena), and novel viewpoints. Traditional experimental (empirical, statistical, etc.) methods find their way into the methodology of some transpersonalists, particularly in the case of the investigation of psi phenomena. With respect to theoretical transpersonal psychology, observation and analysis of human behavior has led to the formulation or recognition of specific constructs that are used to describe and account for the various manifestations of human personality and the larger construct of the self.

Transpersonal psychology relies on the so-called scientific method as much as possible, but its practitioners do not permit the inherent limitation of supposed scientific rigor to constrain its conceptual horizons and ideas about what may or may not be true. Where it is possible for them to lend their support to an idea or theory, statistical and other forms of empirical proof are welcomed. Many transpersonalists accept the idea, that is the intuition, as real enough or worthy enough to trigger an investigation or discuss a reality grounded in ancient traditional beliefs. Other transpersonalists may experience the truth of the idea as being so intense or so real that the experience itself becomes the final indicator of its validity. The situation is illustrated by the following "description of space-time by the Buddhist master Suzuki with that first introduced into physics by Hermann Minkowski in 1908. Suzuki is first (Walsh, 1980, p. 671).

> We look around and perceive that . . . every object is related to every other object . . . not only spatially but temporally . . . As a fact of pure experience, there is no space without time, no time without space; they are interpenetrating. (Suzuki, 1959, p. 33)[3]

> The views of space and time which I wish to lay before you have sprung from the soil of experimental physics, and therein lies their strength. They are radical. Henceforth space by itself, and time by itself, are doomed to fade away into mere shadow, and only a kind of union of the two will preserve an independent reality. (Einstein, 1923, p. 75)

Transpersonal psychology offers itself as one type of solution to the existentialist's search for meaning. It offers, among other things, the spiritual path or path of entry to higher realms of being, knowing, and communicating. The subareas that comprise the discipline of transpersonal psychology include traditionally classified religious disciplines such as Zen Buddhism and the more ancient practices of applied alchemy and astrological concepts (Tart, 1975). Transpersonal psychology also identifies other paths of entry to higher levels of consciousness that are grounded in modern consciousness-raising applications of

Western biological sciences, such as biofeedback. Sutich (1969) suggests the range of topics covered by transpersonal psychology. However, the most important aspect of the definition of transpersonal psychology presented is the way in which its content is to be interpreted.

Any paper written on the vast topic of transpersonal psychology should be very clear with regards to how its subject matter is being interpreted. As presented in this writing, transpersonal psychology is primarily interpreted as a psychology with strong consciousness expanding, spiritual, theistic, supernatural, or psi overtones; however, this is not to deny the usefulness of any naturalistic interpretation of transpersonal phenomena.

Some transpersonal psychologists study consciousness experiences that are typically extraordinary (e.g., the experience of a God-Force, out-of-body experience, etc.). The answer to the question, "Do transpersonalists personally believe in these phenomena?," depends on the transpersonalist being questioned. It is reasonable to believe that many do. They are not unlike practitioners and investigators of behavioral, psychoanalytic, or humanistic-existential psychology who in turn may have extremely strong personal beliefs in the tenets and/or subject matter of their respective psychological orientation.

The sensation-oriented psychologist who strongly adheres to many of the tenets of logical positivism would have the most difficult time accepting or possibly understanding the more profound nature of transpersonal psychology. Thinking- and feeling-oriented psychologists may be intrigued by the subject matter of transpersonal psychology, but neither is likely to embrace its doctrines without careful and prolonged evaluations of its topic areas. The sensation, thinking, and feeling functions are useful but limited in helping humans find answers to their most enduring spiritual concerns. It takes a highly developed intuitive function to tap into the realm of ideas and the realm of hidden essences where, perhaps, answers can be found. Neither transpersonal psychology nor so-called pure intuition is viewed with high respect within American psychology. Transpersonal psychology is the inferior psychology: it is the vehicle of expression for the inferior function in American psychology.

The hypothesized relationship between the psychological functions and four psychological forces with respect to one aspect of the fourfold structure of the psyche of American psychology is depicted diagrammatically in Figure 2-2 based on the above analysis.

Position of the Superior
Force-Function

Behavioral-Sensation Psychology

Position of the First
Auxiliary Force-Function

Position of the Second
Auxiliary Force-Function

Psychoanalytic-Thinking
Psychology

Humanistic-Existential-
Feeling Psychology

Position of the Inferior
Force-Function

Transpersonal-Intuitive Psychology

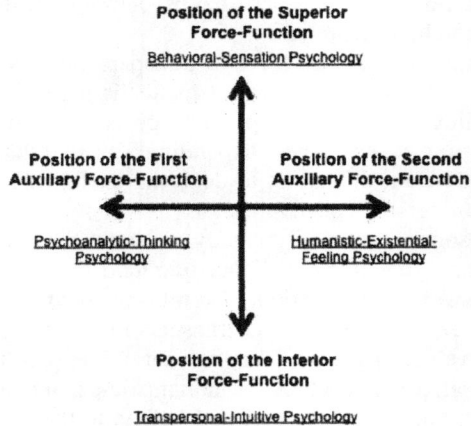

Figure 2-2 Hypothesized relationship between the four
psychological functions and four related psychologies in the psyche
of American psychology.

In 1931, Jung wrote the following passage about the purpose of each psychological function:

> Sensation establishes what is actually present, thinking enables us to recognize
> its meaning, feeling tells us its value, and intuition points to possibilities as to
> whence it came and whither it is going. (pp. 540-541)

Substituting the four functions with their respective psychology, as suggested in
Jung's analysis, provides an encapsulating statement about the nature of a psychology that draws on all aspects of the four psychological functions. Jung's
passage rewritten with the substitutions becomes:

> Sensation/behavioral psychologies establish what is actually present,[4] thinking/psychoanalytic psychologies enable us to recognize (our) meaning[5], feeling/humanistic-existential psychologies tell us (our) values[6], and intuitive/
> transpersonal psychologies point to possibilities as to whence (we) came and
> whither (we) are going[7].

Many persons are seeking answers to the question, "Where is humankind going?" or "What is my purpose in life?" A psychology that can help us answer these and similar questions is clearly worthy of our most serious attention.

Notes

1.   Excerpted from Jennings, G-H. (1982) doctoral dissertation.
2.   To be used interchangeably with psychoanalysis and Freudian psychology.
3.   This Buddhist concept is ancient.
4.   They identify those aspects of who we are that can readily be observed and/or measured.
5.   They explain the mechanisms that account for our functioning or provide etiological interpretations of our actions or our behaviors.
6.   They identify our worth, our importance and the things that are important to us.
7.   They help us identify what one might call our "true origin," our essential purpose or our ultimate or transcendent destination.

Chapter 3
The Role of the Inferior Function in Jungian Psychology

"The individual may strive after perfection but must suffer from the opposite of his intentions for the sake of his completeness."
C. G. Jung, "Aion" in *Collected Works*

Although it is grounded in the unconscious realm of the Jungian Model of the psyche, the fourth function takes form in opposition to the first function that develops and influences consciousness. The fourth function is also known as the inferior function because any attempts on its part to differentiate or develop can only occur after similar and usually far more successful attempts by the first (superior), second (first auxiliary), and third (second auxiliary) functions.

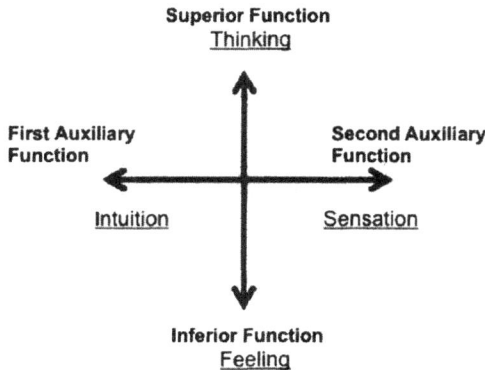

Superior Function
Thinking

First Auxiliary
Function

Second Auxiliary
Function

Intuition

Sensation

Inferior Function
Feeling

Figure 3-1 An aspect of the fourfold structure of the psyche depicting a possible arrangement of the psychological functions.

Adding further thoughts from Jung (1923),

> Experience shows that it is practically impossible, owing to adverse cir-
> cumstances in general, for anyone to develop all his psychological functions
> simultaneously. The demands of society compel a man to apply himself first
> and foremost to the differentiation of the function with which he is best
> equipped by nature, or which will secure him the greatest social success. Very
> frequently, indeed as a general rule, a man identifies more or less completely
> with the most favoured and hence the most developed function . . . As a conse-
> quence of this one-sided development, one or more functions are necessarily re-
> tarded. These functions may properly be called inferior in a psychological but
> not psychopathological sense, since they are in no way morbid but merely
> backward as compared with the favoured function. (p. 450)

Unlike the other functions, which typically serve the will of the person's
ego, the inferior function is permeated with great power that seemingly creates a
direction or has a will of its own. It can be experienced as "the hated trouble-
some or silly thing," or "the thing one does not like to do or cannot do well," or
as the "thing that fascinates one," even though the reasons underlying the fasci-
nation are not always clear. Still everyone is inclined to devalue his or her inferior function at one time or another, not realizing that this function is potentially
the most powerful and may do the most good for the individual in the long run.
von Franz (1971) addresses this point when she writes:

> The behavior of the inferior function is wonderfully mirrored in those
> fairy tales where there is the following structure. A king has three sons. He
> likes the two older sons but the youngest is regarded as a fool. The King then
> sets a task in which the sons may have to find the water of life, or the most
> beautiful bride, or chase away a secret enemy who every night steals the horses
> or the golden apples out of the royal garden. Generally the two elder sons set
> out and get nowhere or get stuck, and then the third saddles his horse while
> everybody laughs and tells him he'd better stay at home by the stove where he
> belongs. But it is usually he who performs the great task. This fourth figure–the
> third in the story, but the fourth figure in the setup–has, according to the myths,
> different superficial qualities. Sometimes he is the youngest, sometimes he is a
> bit idiotic, and sometimes he is a complete fool. (p. 6)

For an individual, that "great task" can be and often is the movement of the person towards a greater sense of wholeness or completion.

The myth of the king and his three sons reveals the power, frustration, or
fulfillment inherent in the inferior function. In the myth, one notes that there is
the King (the first figure in the story) who is wise and capable, but only to a

certain point. It soon becomes apparent that, although he is knowledgeable and consequently capable of mapping out a seemingly sound strategy that allows him to identify and approach the task at hand, he is incapable of completing the task by himself. The king yields to the actions of others, his sons, not because they are as good as he is, but because they act out effective goal oriented strategies. All along it is obvious that there is similarity among the first three figures in myths of this type. Though not co-equals, the first three figures emerge as members of a select group within which the fourth is not invited to join.

Try as they might, the king's first two sons (second and third figures in the story), like the King himself, reach a point where it becomes obvious to them and/or to others that the goal is slipping away or is incapable of being accomplished. Neither the king nor his two sons in stories of this type seriously consider asking the third son (fourth figure in the story) for assistance that might lead to the achievement of the great goal. In fact, they are more likely to actively bar the fourth figure from working on the task. No one really believes the fourth figure in the story has any talent so worthwhile that he can do what the three other figures obviously cannot do.

The three often join together in a common attitude or action against the one. Or the three share one or more common qualities that permit the claim that they are better than the fourth.

A myth with similar characters consistent with the ideas expressed so far might include a wise King or any Head of State who dresses in golden armor or robes. This first figure recognizes the power of a knight who dresses in silver garments, and he may form a partnership with him. These two may broaden the partnership to include a third figure, usually a second knight who dresses in bronze. These three share a splendor that is far greater than the "silly little knight" who eventually comes along, but who dresses himself in tin.

Another way in which characters play out the above pattern can be seen in myths in which the head of a household (and it could be a man or a woman) has two mature children, usually two sons or two daughters, and one immature son or daughter. Sometimes the immaturity of the fourth figure refers to his or her age, but in other stories it refers to his or her mental state. Everything about the first three figures is better than the fourth: they look better, they have better ideas, better clothes, better manners, and so forth. But when the opportunity comes for the greatest success, the first three figures stand shocked as they watch the fourth figure succeed in his or her efforts to attain the goal that the others tried to achieve. The three nearly always believe that the fourth figure is simply not good enough to help them, and this is usually their mistake.

Prior to his or her success, the fourth figure is found living in the hole in the floor or in the tiny room off to the side, or he or she is covered with soot or dresses in rags. The image clearly is of one who is woefully inadequate. Occasionally, he is viewed as someone who at best can provide a few good laughs. Yet interestingly, one finds that occasionally the third figure reveals a sympathetic attitude towards the fourth figure. For in some myths of this kind, prior to the arrival of the fourth figure, it is the third figure who is viewed as having room to grow or still needing to mature just a little more to be the equal or near equal of the first two. The arrival of the fourth figure often takes the focus off of the third figure and/or makes the third figure look better.

In most of the myths, few are shown to recognize the promise embodied by the fourth. Moreover, when the promise of the fourth is noted, it is least likely to be recognized by the first figure. The first figure always offers the greatest opposition to the fourth. Even when the promise and necessary skills to achieve a task are clearly visible in the fourth figure, often denial or rationalizations are used to account for his or her success, for example, she was lucky.

The grouping of the three that are similar against the one appears in various forms in myths and fairy tales. As in the story of *Goldilocks and the Three Bears*, sometimes the identity of the fourth figure is a real mystery to the other three, leading characters to declare, "somebody was eating my porridge, sitting in my chair, or sleeping in my bed." When the fourth figure is finally encountered, the three are shocked into the realization that someone quite different from them can have such an upsetting effect on their experience, or be such a force in their world, and fear abounds. In another popular fairy tale, *The Three Little Pigs*, the three unite to destroy the fourth figure depicted as a wolf who seeks to consume the three pigs, if given the chance. In yet another fairy tale *Cinderella,* the fourth figure, Cinderella, stands in opposition to the group of three comprised of her stepmother and two stepsisters who believe they can have a happy life without her, only to discover much later that their harsh treatment of Cinderella denies them the happiness and success they sought.

These are but a few examples wherein one can see that integrating the fourth figure with the other three becomes impossible. Integration can only happen after a shift or transformation in awareness occurs that involves an embracing, recognition, and acceptance of the value and/or power of the fourth by the other three. The ideal would be for the four to operate in greater harmony with each other when the group of three figures and the one figure stand in the presence of each other. But that can never be guaranteed. Major questions arise: Will they, can they, or should they integrate to form a collective whole? Indeed what price, if any, must be paid for failure to integrate? This is, in effect, the problem of the three and the one.

In all of the examples cited above, the fourth figure is in some way synonymous with the inferior function. Parallels drawn between the fourth figure in the examples given and the inferior function in the psyche of an individual suggest multiple possible outcomes. In the story of the King and his three sons, the realization that the fourth son can help the other three occurs only after much frustration, rejection, and denial. The realization makes what was previously understated obvious and important; the three and the one are part of the same whole or family. The most difficult tasks can be achieved when they recognize the value of each other and the support that they can give each other. In such a case, all figures attain success because the common goal is achieved.

Chapter 4
One of These Psychologies Is Unlike the Others

"Complete human beings are exceptions."
C. G. Jung, "Psychology and Religion" in *Collected Works*

American psychology has a psyche of its own that is distinct from a European, African, or Far Eastern psyche; and although it is not a person, American psychology was born at a certain moment in time and space. From its earliest beginnings, much confusion and energy have been invested in bitter conflicts over the various psychological approaches that mirror viewpoints of the person and the methods used in exploring the person. Nowhere is this reflected more strongly than in the area of personality theory. Different explanations for the existence of the theories, and various summaries aimed at comprehending the differing and at times competing or conflicting psychological viewpoints, or methodologies have been offered. Frager and Fadiman (2005) take the position that there is "no single truth" regarding how we look at personality, rather "various theories employ differing fundamental assumptions and dissimilar data. It is not surprising, therefore, that they come to different conclusions" (p. 6). Still, Hall and Lindzey (1985) write, "personality theories can usefully be understood and compared in terms of nine basic issues that confront modern theorists." They offer examples including conscious versus unconscious and heredity versus environment, and further add, "Most theorists take positions that fall somewhere on the continua along which these dimensions of personality theory lie, but some strongly emphasize one or the other of the stated poles" (p. 22). Ellenberger (1970) argues that the ideas presented by many of the leading theorists reflect their "own struggle to understand human nature" and may in fact emerge as a creative attempt to work through the theorist's own psychopathology. Monte (1991) writes that personality theories represent, "psychohistory, illuminated by the human character of its creators and opaqued by the character of their human limits" (p. 10). Engler (2009) states, "there is no one scientific method, philosophical approach, or psychotherapeutic strategy that would serve as an adequate model for all others" (p. 22), but that each of the theories offers its own measure of science, philosophy, and art.

Ewen (1993) points out that the theorists are trying to comprehend human nature at its most fundamental level. He goes on to write, "There is as yet no one best theory of personality, and the great psychologists whose views we will examine frequently disagree with one another" (p. 3). In *Theories of Personality: A Zonal Perspective*, Berecz (2009) identifies "personality zones" as a way of understanding the theories. He writes:

A personality zone is a conceptual "work space" located at a particular intersection of the vertical axis (molecular > macro) and the horizontal axis (self > other). From a vertical perspective, personality is seen as operating somewhere between the biochemical micro-infinities below and the astrophysical macro-infinities above. We live our lives sandwiched between two universes, both out of reach of our complete understanding.

From a horizontal perspective, self and situations blend imperceptibly into one another, so that at times we feel as if we are in charge of our lives, while at other times we feel dominated by our circumstances. By anchoring personality theories in particular zones we can more easily make sense of their constructs and processes. (p. 5)

The above represents a diverse collection of explanations and accounts given for the current state of personality theories, for the effort at organizing the theories, and employing the methods used to gather information. To expand this complex collection of ideas even further, I offer my own viewpoint: Taken as a whole, the various personality theories in American psychology represent a process of development that can readily be explained by applying the ideas of Jung's type theory. I believe significant insight can be gained by noting the process of differentiation of the four psychological functions within the psyche of American psychology.

There are three strikingly powerful and widely accepted psychological orientations in American psychology that are grounded in three of the Jungian functions. Those three functions are sensation, thinking, and feeling. Monte (1991) refers to the psychological orientations as "the big three–radical behaviorism, classical psychoanalysis, and humanistic psychology." They have also been referred to as the first, second, and third forces in American psychology by leading humanistic theorists (Maslow, 1971; Sutich, 1969). Based on a shared and favored methodology and epistemology, within the domain of the sensation psychologies, in addition to behaviorism are cognitive-behavioral, biological psychologies, statistically based theories (e.g., theories grounded in factor analysis), and debatably, the relatively new positive psychology. Research in these areas depends most heavily on traditional scientific approaches. Among these potent approaches, currently biological psychology seemingly is in the lead with respect to new research findings, growth in literature, and applications.

An examination of the current state of psychoanalytic and humanistic-existential psychologies reveals that they maintain important and meaningful numbers of followers throughout the country. The fundamental tenets of psychoanalytic and humanistic-existential psychologies are viewed as valid across several sub-disciplines in psychology. These psychologies maintain their hard fought for and earned respect. Respect for transpersonal psychology is not as broad in scope. It is a well-known fact that major academic institutions, hospitals, clinics, psychological research centers, and, most notably, psychological conferences are known for advocating one or more particular psychological approaches over others. Comparatively speaking, few of these organizations or their sponsors advocate the transpersonal approach. Psychologists with a strong interest in spirituality and transpersonal psychology seeking tenure at many colleges and universities put their reputations at risk. They may not get tenure or the promotions they might otherwise have achieved if they had produced articles and books in fields of study other than the transpersonal.

Currents of thought in psychology appear to operate within the psyche of American psychology in ways similar to those in which the psychological functions operate within the psyche of the individual. In the individual and in American psychology, a worldview (or in the case of psychology, a methodology or way of knowing) emerges that either is, or tends to be, valued highly over other ways of gathering, construing, or yielding information about the world.

In both the individual and American psychology, there is resistance to accepting a worldview or a manner of knowing that is linked to what Jung would call the inferior function. Things associated with the inferior function are often devalued; and such an attitude typically isolates the worldview associated with the inferior function as well as anything that stems from it. The overall result is that the psyche becomes a battlefield for a dynamic that pits one form of knowledge or understanding against another form. In some cases, after the tension from their initial efforts to live in the same arena has died down, the first three functions, their by-products, and activities, join forces and stand guard against the by-products and activities of the remaining function. In all cases, the first function seeks to dominate in the place where the battle occurs. Among the first three functions, it is the first function that stands most steadfastly against the remaining one. And it is the first function that has the most to lose if the remaining one is allowed to enter the arena and become an active and respected player. Either way, the dynamic, though potentially growth enhancing (assuming that all functions in the end are given the chance to operate appropriately), points to a problem involving significant disharmony.

The differing and at times conflicting theories on human nature offered by psychologists point to a type problem within American psychology. The rejection of the tenets of the transpersonal psychologies by mainstream psychologists who view the tenets of the first three forces as more credible reveals a classic example of the problem of the three and the one. This problem exists in American psychology, and it highlights the view that intuitively based psychologies are fundamentally unlike the others, especially when they advocate tenets that are grounded in the spiritual.

In exploring the whole of American psychology, new students in the discipline might be surprised, if not astounded, by the tremendous differences in the types of literature found in American psychology. Moving from the literature of the sensation oriented behavioral, cognitive-behavioral, biological, statistically based psychologies to the literature of the thinking oriented psychoanalytic or feeling oriented humanistic-existential psychologies, and certainly to the intuitive oriented transpersonal literature is like traveling from one foreign country to another. Each area offers a different terrain: one must know different languages to understand each place, and one tends to experience different aspects of human nature in each location.

At times the literature produced by each function is so different that a student may wonder how the discipline of psychology has found a way to integrate it all to the extent it has. The truth of the matter is that even given its dynamic history of often competing schools, forces, and definitions of psychology, mainstream American psychology has slowly moved towards greater internal harmony and inclusiveness, but only with regards to the tenets of its sensation, thinking, and feeling psychologies. As the psychologies of these functions gain momentum in finding merit in each other, the true and only remaining foreign land becomes the hated or apprehension-inducing domain of the intuitively based psychologies.

American psychologists must consider a commitment to exploring the domain of intuition and the view of the person it produces. But they must recognize that the domain of intuition cannot and must not become a substitute for the domain of sensation. We must accept the intuitive domain for what it is, and for what it has to offer. Our task is to identify and develop appropriate theories that will serve as passages throughout the intuitive domain. Already our efforts at identifying or creating passages through the domains of sensation, thinking, and feeling have revealed a great deal of knowledge about human nature. Yet, there are other places to explore–new passages to follow and identify, if not create.

The reigning forces in American psychology primarily offer materialistic and secular views of the person. One must search long and hard to find spiritual views of human beings in the literature of mainstream psychology. Indeed, there appears to be a great metaphorical wall that separates the materialistic and secular views of human nature from a spiritual one in American psychology. Although there is a gate in the wall that one could conceivably go through in order to explore the other side, upon pressing forward one discovers that the gate is barely ajar. Rather than serving as a deterrent to crossing over to the other side, the heavy gate triggers a determination to summon the necessary strength on the part of the inquisitive and unyielding traveler to open it wider. As the traveler struggles mightily to open the gate wider, and ultimately to the widest degree possible, the following thought becomes etched upon the traveler's mind, "If we ever hope to complete the road map to human nature, we must not only travel and create passages on the familiar side of the gate, we must travel and create passages beyond the gate.

Chapter 5
Towards an American Psychology for All Psychological Types

"If one does not understand a person, one tends to regard him as a fool."
C. G. Jung, "Mysterium Coniunctionis" in *Collected Works*

I have argued (Jennings, 1982) that American psychologists need to formulate and follow through on the efforts required to make American psychology more inclusive of theories and practices that enhance our understanding of transcendence and sharpen our focus on the spiritual nature of human beings. Our present psychological viewpoint of the person largely stems from behavioral, biological, psychodynamic, and humanistic-existential psychological perspectives. Although remarkable in its understanding of many salient aspects of human nature, it is nevertheless incomplete. In articulating the logical links between the four psychological functions in Jungian psychology and the so-called four forces in American psychology, I have isolated and focused on a dynamic that I trust other psychologists will come to believe is worthy of understanding. Specifically, that dynamic explored in a Jungian context identifies the possible role of the inferior function in the psyche of American psychology, and the promise that it offers.

As we continue to look at American psychology through the lens of a Jungian approach, we are presented with an opportunity to view what American psychology can be in the decades to come. As we move more deeply into the third millennium, American psychologists should take note of the discipline's powerful identification with the sensing function. This identification is clearly evident when one looks at the content of the literature that psychologists value most highly as compared to American psychology's extremely weak identification with the literature that stems from what I characterize as its fourth or intuiting function. American psychology must mature to the point where it can detach its ego from an overwhelming identification with sensation, its superior function. In fact, a complete American psychology should be detached from a primary reliance on any single function.

One could ask, how might we characterize an American psychology that achieved the goal of detachment from all functions? von Franz (1971) describes the abilities of some Zen Masters, which I believe can be a model for how American psychology should operate. She points out that without being "inwardly bound to the ego functions he uses in meeting a particular situation" (p.

64), certain Zen Masters are able to apply the appropriate psychological functions to the appropriate tasks or situations at hand.

The type of Zen Master she describes would not feel the need to bring the same primary function to which an attachment has been formed to every situation or person he meets out of fear or ignorance of the others functions, or because he is convinced that his primary function is always the best one to use. A Zen Master, as described above, acts on his flexible application of the functions, consistently employing the use of the most appropriate function for an optimal understanding of the person, event, or situation he encounters.

American psychology cannot hope to provide a deep spiritually and intuitively based understanding of human nature as long as it blocks, denies, or suppresses the full creative expression of intuition in its psyche. The great wall created by the dominance of sensation must be penetrated, because this wall, which was quite helpful in the past, now stands in the way of our gaining necessary knowledge.

Some psychologists will strongly question the value, or at worst, view as completely foolish the psychologies that would result from unbridled intuition; yet these psychologies must be allowed to emerge and develop, even if that development leads to a radical expression of intuition. This would not be any different from how many psychologists past and present view (and have viewed) the radical behaviorism of Watson and Skinner. What should be noted is that, historically speaking, radical sensation-based psychology offered a viewpoint of the person that fostered the development of more integrated approaches, for example, cognitive-behavioral psychology (Bandura and Walters, 1963; Bandura, 1977; Rotter, Chance, and Phares, 1972; Rotter, 1982) and the behavioral psychoanalytic rapprochement found in the psychological theory and methodology of Dollard and Miller (1950).

It appears that a radical expression of a discipline resulting from a psychological function is at times necessary as part of that function's differentiation, that is, its path of separation and distinct development from an immature expression to a more mature one. When this happens in psychology, other functions can then begin to modify the content of the radical psychology produced by the function, and new psychological theories can result from the synthesis. In the long run, psychology as a discipline is likely to benefit from both the radical and modified expressions of all of the psychological functions. Ultimately, these functions can pave the path through dimensions of human experiences and aspects of human nature previously unknown. The future of American psychology and science in general can emerge as a union of science and spirituality as Tart (2009) has argued.

In an attempt to be consistent with interpreting the role of the inferior function in American psychology, I should note that integrating the psychologies grounded in American psychology's inferior function into the mainstream of American psychology would not be easy. But it might be easier than trying to integrate the inferior function into the consciousness of an individual. In individuals, the ego assimilates its first and second functions, and in some cases a third function. This condition represents an optimal state, but it means the fourth function is not readily assimilated and thus, it remains inferior (von Franz, 1971).

In an individual, it is important for the inferior function to remain inferior for it serves as the door to the unconscious through which the archetypes can influence consciousness and facilitate the psychological development of the person. The individual with intuition as his or her inferior function will most likely always have inferior intuition. However, American psychology with intuition as its inferior function can strengthen the role that intuition plays in the discipline to a considerable extent. The strength of intuition in relation to the other three functions can be altered as a result of American psychologists' openness to the creative byproducts and activities of intuition that emerge from individuals who are highly intuitive, as well as from intuitively based traditions.

The psychological theories that are a means of expressions for the tenets of more than one psychological function (e.g., Dollard and Miller's psychodynamic behaviorism) can help different psychological types gain a greater understanding and appreciation of the discipline as a whole. I can recall when I had this experience. For years I had a hard time accepting behavioral based psychologies as meaningful or desirable, and I had the most difficult experience in my attempts to accept even portions of radical behaviorism. However, I learned to appreciate behavioral approaches after making a connection with cognitive-behavioral psychology and social learning theory. My intuiting function would not allow me to readily accept behaviorism, however, I could connect with it through my feeling function in its modified social learning form as represented by the work of Albert Bandura (1977, 1989, 2001, 2006) due to its inclusion of what he would eventually identify as an agentic perspective. Engler (2009) writes:

> Whereas earlier learning theories primarily depended on principles of reinforcement to account for how human behavior is developed or changed, Bandura has increasingly viewed people as agents, or originators, of experience. (p. 235)

That form allowed me to experience an element of humanism in the domain of first force psychology.

Today we find that many Americans are seeking answers to their spiritual concerns. Many have powerful spiritual yearnings. These concerns stem from our spiritual nature. Although in some cases religious tradition and ritual serve to help some people meet these needs, many have noted a glaring gap between spirituality and the way it is practiced by some established religions that demand adherence to specific rules and regulations. The rules, in turn, serve to stifle as opposed to promote personal growth, self-actualization, and/or transcendence. Although psychology cannot be expected to completely meet the spiritual needs of all people, it should be able to provide help to many individuals in spiritual crisis and with spiritual concerns. Some of this work is taking place today, but much more needs to occur. Even though a few authors of personality textbooks (Frager and Fadiman, 2005; Engler, 2009; and Berecz, 2009) have included transpersonal theories or concepts in their publications, a broader effort aimed at including theories, concepts, therapies, and empirical methodologies that explore the transpersonal domain should be integrated into mainstream writings (including mainstream textbooks), and made part of the undergraduate curriculum, graduate curriculum, and professional training of psychologists across the nation. Following the seminal work of Carl G. Jung, several ground-breaking theorists and researchers have, in relatively recent years, contributed to the growing foundation of transpersonal or spiritually related literature (Tart, 1975, 2009; Grof, 1989, 2007; Vaughan, 1971; Myers, 1992; Wilber, 2001; Visser, 2003; Frager and Fadiman, 2005). A few important graduate programs have emerged that serve as models for training and the enhancement of transpersonal education.

We have the opportunity to create an American psychology that delineates human nature in ways that can be widely appreciated and understood by many people. Much of the work that needs to be done to create this more complete psychology, which will be inclusive of the transpersonal domain, will need to be done by many individuals, some of who are today's students. When American psychology moves to the point of embracing intuitively based psychologies, it will truly become a psychology that is expressive of all psychological types.

American psychology offers us a great promise. It is my belief that in the third millennium, American psychology will develop out of the domains of its psychological forces into a creative unified synthesis that will provide noteworthy and balanced expression of all four psychological functions. As the subtle psychological processes that are necessary to bring this about gain momentum, one can be certain that a new but yet to be fully experienced vitality in American psychology awaits all who are drawn to this call for a new openness and synthesis of ideas.

References

Adler, A. (1930). Individual psychology. In C. Muchison (Ed.), *Psychologies of 1930.* Worcester, MA: Clark University Press.

Alfred, A. (1939). *Social interests: A challenge to mankind.* (J. Linton & R. Vaughan, Trans.). New York: Putnam.

Bandura, A., & Walters, R. H. (1963). *Social learning and personality development.* New York: Holt, Rinehart, and Winston.

Bandura, A. (1977). *Social learning theory.* Englewood Cliffs, NJ: Prentice-Hall.

Bandura, A. (1989). Human agency in social cognitive theory. *American Psychologist*, 44, 1175-1184.

Bandura, A. (2001). Social cognitive theory: An agentic perspective. *Annual Review of Psychology*, 52, 1-26.

Bandura, A. (2006). Toward a psychology of human agency. *Perspective on Psychological Science*, 1(2), 164-180.

Beck, A. (1972). *Depression: Causes and treatments.* Philadelphia: University of Pennsylvania Press.

Beck , A. (2005). Cognitive therapy found to cut attempted suicide risk in half. *Mental Health Weekly*, 15(31), 5, 8-9.

Berecz, J. M. (2009). *Theories of Personality: A zonal perspective.* New York: Pearson Allyn & Bacon.

Buss, D. M. (1990). Toward a biologically informed psychology of personality. *Journal of Personality*, 58, 1-16.

Buss, D. M. (1991). Evolutionary personality psychology. *Annual Review of Psychology*, 42, 459-492.

Dollard, J., & Miller, N. E. (1950). *Personality and psychotherapy: An analysis in terms of learning, thinking, and culture.* New York: McGraw-Hill.

Einstein, A. (1923). *The principle of relativity.* New York: Dover.

Ellenberger, H. (1970). *The discovery of the unconscious.* New York: Basic Books.

Engler, B. (2009). *Personality theories: An introduction* (8th Ed.). Boston: Houghton Mifflin.

Ewen, R. B. (1993). *An introduction to theories of personality* (4th Ed.). Hillside, NJ: Lawrence Erlbaum Associates, Publishers.

Eysenck, H. J. (1967). *The biological basis of personality.* Springfield, IL: Charles C. Thomas.

Eysenck, H. J. (1982). *Personality, genetics, and behavior: Selected papers.* New York: Praeger.

Fine, R. (1973). Psychoanalysis. In R. Corsini (Ed.), *Current psychotherapies.* New York: F. E. Peacock.

Frager, R., & Fadiman, J. (2005). *Personality and personal growth* (6th Ed.). Upper Saddle River, NJ: Pearson-Prentice Hall.

Freud, A. (1946). *The ego and the mechanism of defense.* New York: International Universities Press.

Freud, S. (1963). Introductory lectures on psychoanalysis. In J. Strachey (Ed. & Trans.), *The standard edition of the complete psychological works of Sigmund Freud,* Vol. 10. London: Hogarth Press.

Freud, S. (1966). *On the history of the psycho-analytic movement.* New York: W. W. Norton

Gray, H., & Wheelwright, J. B. (1944). Jung's psychological types and marriage. *Stanford Medical Bulletin,* 2.

Gray, H., & Wheelwright. J. B. (1945). Jung's psychological types, including the four functions. *Journal of General Psychology,* 33.

Grof, S. (1989). *Spiritual emergency: When personal transformation becomes a crisis.* Tarcher Press.

Grof, S. (2007). *Ancient wisdom and modern science.* New York: State University of New York Press.

Hall, C. S. & Lindzey, G. (1985). *Introduction to theories of personality.* New York: John Wiley & Sons.

Horney, K. (1939). *New ways in psychoanalysis.* New York: W. W. Norton.

Horney, K. (1945). *Our inner conflicts: A constructive theory of neurosis.* New York: W. W. Norton.

Hull, C. L. (1943). *Principles of behavior: An introduction to behavior theory.* New York: Appleton-Century-Crofts.

James, W. (1902). *The varieties of religious experience: A study in human nature.* New York: Longmans, Green & Co.

Jennings, G-H. (1982). A theory on the relationship between four Jungian functions and four psychological forces: behavioral, psychoanalytic, humanistic-existential, and transpersonal [CD-ROM]. Abstract from: ProQuest File: Dissertation Abstracts Item: 8213316.

Jung, C. G. (1923). *Psychological types or the psychology of individuation.* (H. Godwin Baynes & M. B. B. C. Cantab, Trans.). New York: Harcourt, Brace, & Company, Inc.

Jung, C. G. (1931/1971). A psychological theory of types. In *Collected Works* (Vol. 6). Princeton: Princeton University Press.

Kinget, G. M. (1975). *On being human: A systematic view.* New York: Harcourt-Brace-Jovanovich.

Kohut, H. (1977). *The restoration of the self.* New York: International Universities Press.

Kubie, L. S. (1953). Psychoanalysis as a basic science. In F. Alexander and H. Ross (Eds.), *Twenty years of psycho-analysis.* New York: W. W. Norton.

Lazarus. A .A. (1971). *Behavior therapy and beyond.* New York: McGraw-Hill.

Lazarus, A. A. (1976). *Multimodal behavior therapy.* New York: Springer.

Maddi, S. R. (1976). *Personality theories: A comparative analysis* (3rd ed.) Illinois: Dorsey Press.

Maslow, A. H. (1962/1968). *Toward a psychology of being.* Princeton, NJ: Van Nostrand.

Maslow, A. H. (1964). *Religions, values, and peak experiences.* Columbus, OH: Ohio University Press.

Maslow, A. H. (1971). *The farther reaches of human nature.* New York: Viking Press.

Mischel, W. (1976). *Introduction to personality.* New York: Holt, Rinehart & Winston, Inc.

Monte, C. F. (1991). *Beneath the mask: An introduction to theories of personality* (4th Ed.) Forth Worth, TX: Holt, Rinehart & Winston, Inc.

Myers, L. J. (1992). Transpersonal psychology: The role of the Afrocentric paradigm. In A. K. H. Burlew, W. C. Banks, H. P. McAdoo & D. A. Azibo (Eds.). *African American Psychology.* Newbury Park, CA: Sage Publications.

O'Connell, V., & O'Connell, A. (1974). *Choice and change: An introduction to the psychology of growth.* Englewood Cliffs, NJ: Prentice-Hall, Inc.

Pine, F. (1988). The four psychologies of psychoanalysis and their place in clinical work. *Journal of the American Psychoanalytic Association, 36,* 571-596.

Rogers, C. R. (1951). *Client-centered therapy: Its current practice, implications, and theory.* Boston: Houghton Mifflin.

Rogers, C. R. (1980). *A way of being.* Boston: Houghton Mifflin.

Rotter, J. B. (1966). Generalized expectancies for internal versus external control of reinforcement. *Psychological Monographs, 81.*

Rotter, J. B. (1982). *The development and application of social learning theory: Selected papers.* New York: Praeger.

Rotter, J. B., Chance, J. E., & Phares, E. J. (1972). *Applications of a social learning theory of personality.* New York: Holt, Rhinehart, & Winston.

Seligman, M. E. P. (1975). *Helplessness: On depression, development, and death.* San Francisco: W. H. Freeman.

Seligman, M. E. P. (2006). *Learned optimism: How to change your mind and your life.* New York: Pocket Books.

Seligman, M. E. P. & Csikszentmihalyi, M. (2000). Positive psychology: An introduction. *American Psychologist, 55*(1), 5-14.

Skinner, B. F. (1971). *Beyond freedom and dignity.* New York: Bantam.

Skinner, B. F. (1974). *About Behaviorism.* New York: Alfred A. Knopf.

Spence, K. W. (1948). The postulates and methods of 'behaviorism.' *Psychological Review, 55.*

Sutich, A. J. (1963). *American Association for Humanistic Psychology: Articles of Association.* Palo Alto, CA: Mimeographed, August.

Sutich, A. J. (1969). *Journal of Transpersonal Psychology.*

Suzuki, D. T. (1959). Preface. In B. L. Suzuki, *Mahayana Buddhism.* London: Allen and Unwin.

Tart, C. (1975). *Transpersonal psychologies.* New York: Harper & Row.

Tart, C. (2009). *The end of materialism: How evidence of the paranormal is bringing science and spirit together.* Oakland, CA: New Harbinger Publications, Inc.

Vaughan, F. (2001). *The inward arc: Healing in psychotherapy and spirituality.* iUniverse, Inc.

Visser, F. (2003). *Ken Wilber: Thought as passion.* Albany: State University of New York Press

von Franz, M-L. (1971). The inferior function. In M-L. von Franz & J. Hillman. *Jung's typology.* Zurich, Switzerland: Spring Publications.

Walsh, R. (1980). The consciousness disciplines and the behavioral sciences: Questions of comparison and assessment. *American Journal of Psychiatry,* 137, 6.

Watson, J. B. (1913). Psychology as the behaviorist views it. *The Psychological Review,* 20.

Wilber, K. (2001). *No boundary: Eastern and Western approaches to personal growth.* Shambhala Press.

Yalom, I. D. (1972). Existential factors in (group) psychotherapy. In O. L. McCabe (Ed.), *Changing human behavior: Current therapies and future directions.* New York: Grune & Stratton.

Yarock, S. R. (1993). Understanding chronic bulimia: A four psychologies approach. *The American Journal of Psychoanalysis* Vol. 53, No 1.

Index

Adler, A., 3, 13
Agentic perspective, 37
Alchemy, applied, 18
American psychology, xi, 3, 10; of all
    psychological types, 35–38; domi-
    nance of sensation in, 35–36;
    functions and, 12, 15, 17, 19–20,
    20f, 29–33; psyche of, 29–33;
    theories and psychologies in, 3–4,
    30; types problem within, 3, 31–
    32
Astrological concepts, 18
Auxiliary functions, 6f, 9; of American
    psychology, 15, 17, 20f

Bandura, A., 11, 37
Behavioral psychoanalytical rap-
    prochement, 36
Behavioral psychology: cognitive-, ix,
    11, 30; feeling function and, 12–
    13; intuition function and, 12;
    "methodological," 11; in psyche of
    American psychology, 30; radical
    and moderate, 11–12, 36; sensa-
    tion function paired with, 10–13,
    30; thinking function and, 12–13
Berecz, J. M., 30
Biofeedback, 19
Biological psychology, ix, 11, 30
Buddhism, 18; Zen Masters of, 35–36

Cinderella, 26
Cognitive-behavioral psychology, ix,
    11, 30

Dollard, J., 10, 36–37

Einstein, A., 18

Ellenberger, H., 29
Engler, B., 29, 37
Erickson, E., 13
Evaluative functions, 6–8, 12
Ewen, R. B., 29–30
Existential thought, 16. See also Hu-
    manistic-existential psychology
Extraversion, 5; Freud and, 10

Fadiman, J., 29, 38
Fairy tales, inferior function and, 24–27
Feeling function, 7–9; behavioral psy-
    chology and, 12–13; humanistic-
    existential psychology paired with,
    10, 15–17; psychoanalytic psy-
    chology and, 14; transpersonal
    psychology and, 19
Fine, R., 14
Frager, R., 29, 38
Freud, A., 2
Freud, S., xi, 3, 10; psychoanalytical
    theory and, 13–14
Fromm, E., 13
Functions of consciousness, 5–13, 6f;
    American psychology and, 12, 15,
    17, 19–20, 20f; auxiliary, 6f, 9;
    evaluative, 6–8, 12; flexible appli-
    cation of, 36; operation of, 8–10;
    perceptual, 5, 7–8, 12; rational and
    irrational, 5–6; superior and infe-
    rior, 6f, 8–9; theories expressing
    more than one, 37. See also Feel-
    ing function; Intuition function;
    Sensation function; Thinking
    function

Goldilocks and the Three Bears, 26
Grof, S., 38

Hall, C. S., 29
Hartmann, H., 13
Horney, K., 2, 13
Hull, C. L., 10
Humanistic-existential psychology:
    feeling function paired with, 10,
    15–17; in psyche of American
    psychology, 30–31; sensation
    function and, 15; thinking function
    and, 15

Inferences, 12
Inferior function, 6f, 8–9; in American
    psychology, 19, 20f, 35–38; in
    fairy tales, 24–27; in Jungian psy-
    chology, 23–27, 37; resistance to,
    31
Introversion, 5
Intuition function, 7–8; American psy-
    chology and, 36–38; behavior
    psychology and, 12; passages in
    domain of, 32–33; psychoanalytic
    psychology and, 14–15; transper-
    sonal psychology paired with, 10,
    17–19
Irrational functions, 5. See also Percep-
    tual functions

Jennings, G-H., 4, 35
Judgment. See Evaluative functions
Jung, C. G., x, 1, 5, 7, 29, 35; American
    psychology view of, 3; four func-
    tions and, 9, 20, 23–24; psycho-
    analytical theory and, 13
Jungian ways of knowing, 5–21; evalu-
    ative functions in, 6–8, 12; extra-
    version and introversion in, 5; four
    functions of consciousness in, 5–
    13, 6f; perceptual functions in, 5,
    7–8, 12

Kinget, G. M., 16
Kohut, H., 2
Kubie, L. S., 14

Lindzey, G., 29

Maddi, S. R., 10, 13
Maslow, A. H., ix–x, 10, 13, 15
May, R., ix
Miller, N. E., 10, 36–37
Minkowski, H., 18
Mischel, W., xii, 10–12
Monte, C. F., 29–30
Myers, L. J., 38

Neo-Freudian theorists/psychology, 2,
    13

Object relations theory, 2, 13
Observation: in behavioral psychology,
    11; in psychoanalytical psychol-
    ogy, 13
O'Connell, V. and O'Connell A., 7

Passages: in intuition domain, 32–33;
    as metaphor, ix
Pavlov, I. P., 11
Pennsylvania State University, 1, 3
Perceptual functions, 5, 7–8, 12
Personality theory, xi–xii, 29–30; Jun-
    gian types and, 30–33
"Personality zones," 30
Pine, F., 2
Positive psychology, ix, 30
Psyche, structure of, 6, 6f, 9
Psychic determination principle, 14
Psychoanalytic psychology: feeling
    function and, 14; intuition func-
    tion and, 14–15; in psyche of
    American psychology, 30–31;
    sensation function and, 14; think-
    ing function paired with, 10, 13–
    15; types of, 2, 13
Psychodynamic theorists, 13, 37
Psychological types, problem of, 3, 31–
    32. See also functions of con-
    sciousness

Psychology: radical expressions of, 36; secular and materialistic views of, x–xi. See also American psychology; Behavioral psychology; Biological psychology; Humanistic-existential psychology; Positive psychology; Psychoanalytic psychology; Transpersonal psychology

Radical behavioral psychology, 11–12
Rank, O., 13
Rapaport, D., 13
Rational functions, 5–6. See also Perceptual functions
Rogers, C. R., ix
Rotter, J. B., 12

Schisms in American psychology, 3
Self-theory, 13
Sensation function, 7, 12; behavioral psychology paired with, 10–13, 30; dominance of, in American psychology, 35–36; humanistic psychology and, 15; psychoanalytic psychology and, 14; transpersonal psychology and, 19
Skinner, B. F., x, 10–11
Social learning theory, 37
Spence, K. W., 10
Spirituality, x–xi; mainstream psychology and, 3, 32–33, 37–38
Statistically based theories, 30
Sullivan, H. S., 13
Superior function, 6f, 8–9; American psychology and, 12, 20f, 35
Sutich, A. J., 4, 13, 16–19
Suzuki, D. T., 18

Tart, C., 18, 36, 38
Thinking function, 6, 8–9; behavioral psychology and, 12–13; Freud's extraverted, 10; humanistic psychology and, 15; psychoanalytic psychology paired with, 10, 13–15; transpersonal psychology and, 19
Three and the one, problem of the, 26–27; in American psychology, 32
Three Little Pigs, The, 26
Transcendence, x, 35. See also Spirituality
Transpersonal psychology: feeling function and, 19; integration of, into mainstream writings, 38; intuition function paired with, 10, 17–19; lack of respect for, 31; overlapped with humanistic-existential psychology, 16–17; in psyche of American psychology, 31–33; psychoanalytic psychology and, 14–15; sensation function and, 19; thinking function and, 19
Type problems, 3, 31–32

Vaughan, F., 38
von Franz, M-L., 9; on inferior function, 24, 37; on Zen Masters, 35–36

Walters, R. H., 11
Watson, J. B., 10–11
Western psychological thought, ix
Wilber, K., 38

Yale University, 1–3
Yalom, I. D., 16
Yarock, S. R., 2

Zen Buddhism, 18; Masters, 35–36

About the Author

Before earning his PhD in psychology at The Pennsylvania State University in University Park, PA, George-Harold Jennings was a pre-doctoral fellow in clinical psychology at Yale School of Medicine. Currently, he is a member of the Department of Psychology and a staff psychologist at the McClintock Center for Counseling and Psychological Services at Drew University in Madison, New Jersey.

www.ingramcontent.com/pod-product-compliance
Lightning Source LLC
Chambersburg PA
CBHW030657270326
41929CB00007B/408